T5-COA-117

APPLE BOOKS

College Football Teams North Star Editions

8 – Title Set:	☐	$199.60
Single title:		$24.95
9798892507103	_____	Alabama Crimson Tide
9798892507110	_____	Georgia Bulldogs
9798892507127	_____	Michigan Wolverines
9798892507134	_____	Notre Dame Fighting Irish
9798892507141	_____	Ohio State Buckeyes
9798892507158	_____	Oklahoma Sooners
9798892507165	_____	Texas Longhorns
9798892507172	_____	USC Trojans

TEXAS LONGHORNS

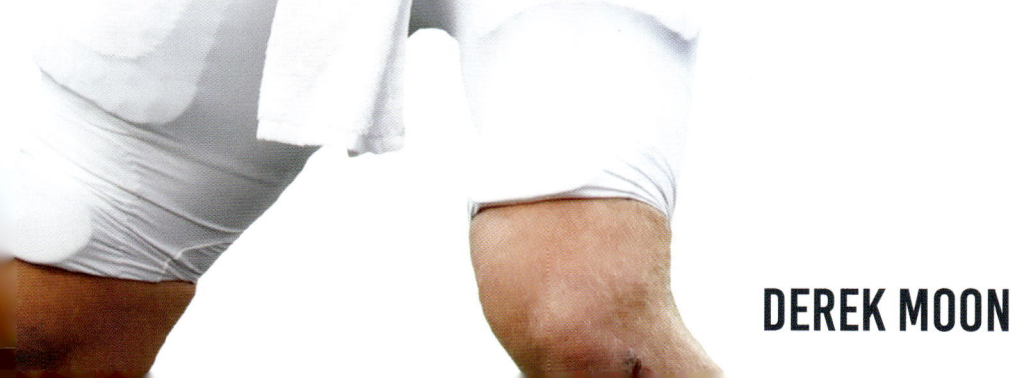

DEREK MOON

WWW.APEXEDITIONS.COM

Copyright © 2026 by Apex Editions, Mendota Heights, MN 55120. All rights reserved. No part of this book may be reproduced or utilized in any form or by any means without written permission from the publisher.

Apex is distributed by North Star Editions:
sales@northstareditions.com | 888-417-0195

Produced for Apex by Red Line Editorial.

Photographs ©: Stephanie Tacy/Sipa USA/AP Images, cover, 1; Cooper Neill/Getty Images Sport/Getty Images, 4–5; David Buono/Icon Sportswire/AP Images, 6–7, 58–59; Shutterstock Images, 8–9; BES/AP Images, 10–11; Bettmann/Getty Images, 12–13; Sam C. Pierson Jr./Houston Chronicle/AP Images, 14–15; Paul Spinelli/AP Images, 16–17; UPI/Bettmann Archive/Getty Images, 19; AP Images, 20–21, 22–23, 24–25; Ted Powers/AP Images, 26–27; Eric Gay/AP Images, 29, 57; Jed Jacobsohn/Getty Images Sport/Getty Images, 30–31; Scott Clarke/WireImage/Getty Images, 32–33; Matt Slocum/AP Images, 34–35; Tim Warner/Getty Images Sport/Getty Images, 36–37, 48–49, 50–51, 52–53, 54–55; Ronald Martinez/Getty Images Sport/Getty Images, 38–39, 40–41; Brian Bahr/Getty Images Sport/Getty Images, 42–43; Alex Slitz/Getty Images Sport/Getty Images, 44–45; Allen Kee/WireImage/Getty Images, 47

Library of Congress Control Number: 2025930931

ISBN
979-8-89250-716-5 (hardcover)
979-8-89250-768-4 (paperback)
979-8-89250-751-6 (ebook pdf)
979-8-89250-734-9 (hosted ebook)

Printed in the United States of America
Mankato, MN
082025

NOTE TO PARENTS AND EDUCATORS

Apex books are designed to build literacy skills in striving readers. Exciting, high-interest content attracts and holds readers' attention. The text is carefully leveled to allow students to achieve success quickly.

TABLE OF CONTENTS

CHAPTER 1
HORNS UP! 4

CHAPTER 2
EARLY HISTORY 8

PLAYER SPOTLIGHT
EARL CAMPBELL 18

CHAPTER 3
LEGENDS 20

PLAYER SPOTLIGHT
RICKY WILLIAMS 28

CHAPTER 4
RECENT HISTORY 30

CHAPTER 5
MODERN STARS 38

PLAYER SPOTLIGHT
VINCE YOUNG 46

CHAPTER 6
TEAM TRIVIA 48

TEAM RECORDS • 56
TIMELINE • 58
COMPREHENSION QUESTIONS • 60
GLOSSARY • 62
TO LEARN MORE • 63
ABOUT THE AUTHOR • 63
INDEX • 64

CHAPTER 1

HORNS UP!

The sun shines down on Austin, Texas. The Longhorn Band blasts "Texas Fight." The fans rise to their feet. Everyone is wearing orange and white. It's game day at the University of Texas!

The Longhorn Band plays at every Texas home game. The band has more than 300 members.

The Texas Longhorns need a big play. The fans hold up their hands. Their fingers stick up like horns. The quarterback takes the snap. He looks to his right. Then he throws a no-look pass up the middle. It's a touchdown! The Longhorns are on their way to another win.

HOOK 'EM HORNS

In 1955, Texas had a big game coming up. Cheerleader Harley Clark wanted to support the team. He came up with the "Hook 'em Horns" symbol. It's now a tradition for Texas fans.

The University of Texas has more than 50,000 students.

CHAPTER 2

EARLY HISTORY

The University of Texas opened in 1883. Its football team started 10 years later. Texas finished the 1893 season 4–0. The team's winning ways continued. For 40 years, Texas never had a losing season.

The University of Texas campus is located in the city of Austin.

Dana X. Bible posted a record of 63–31–3 as the coach of Texas.

Texas hired coach Dana X. Bible in 1937. By then, college football was a major sport. Bible's teams didn't play with much flair. But they won a lot. Bible led Texas to its first No. 1 ranking. He also led the team to its first bowl game. Over Bible's 10 seasons, Texas became a national power.

WHY THE LONGHORNS?

The first Texas teams were called "Varsity." In the early 1900s, the student newspaper introduced "Longhorns." The nickname stuck. Texas longhorns are a type of beef cattle.

The Longhorns finished 10–1 in 1947. But success eventually slipped away. By 1956, they went 1–9. It was the worst record in school history. The team needed a change. Texas turned to up-and-coming coach Darrell K Royal in 1957. That began the program's most successful period.

THE EYES OF TEXAS

A Texas student wrote "The Eyes of Texas" in 1903. It became the school's official song. However, many people say the song is racist. In 2020, Texas players asked the school to stop using it. But in 2021, the school decided to keep the song.

Darrell K Royal became known for using a formation called the wishbone.

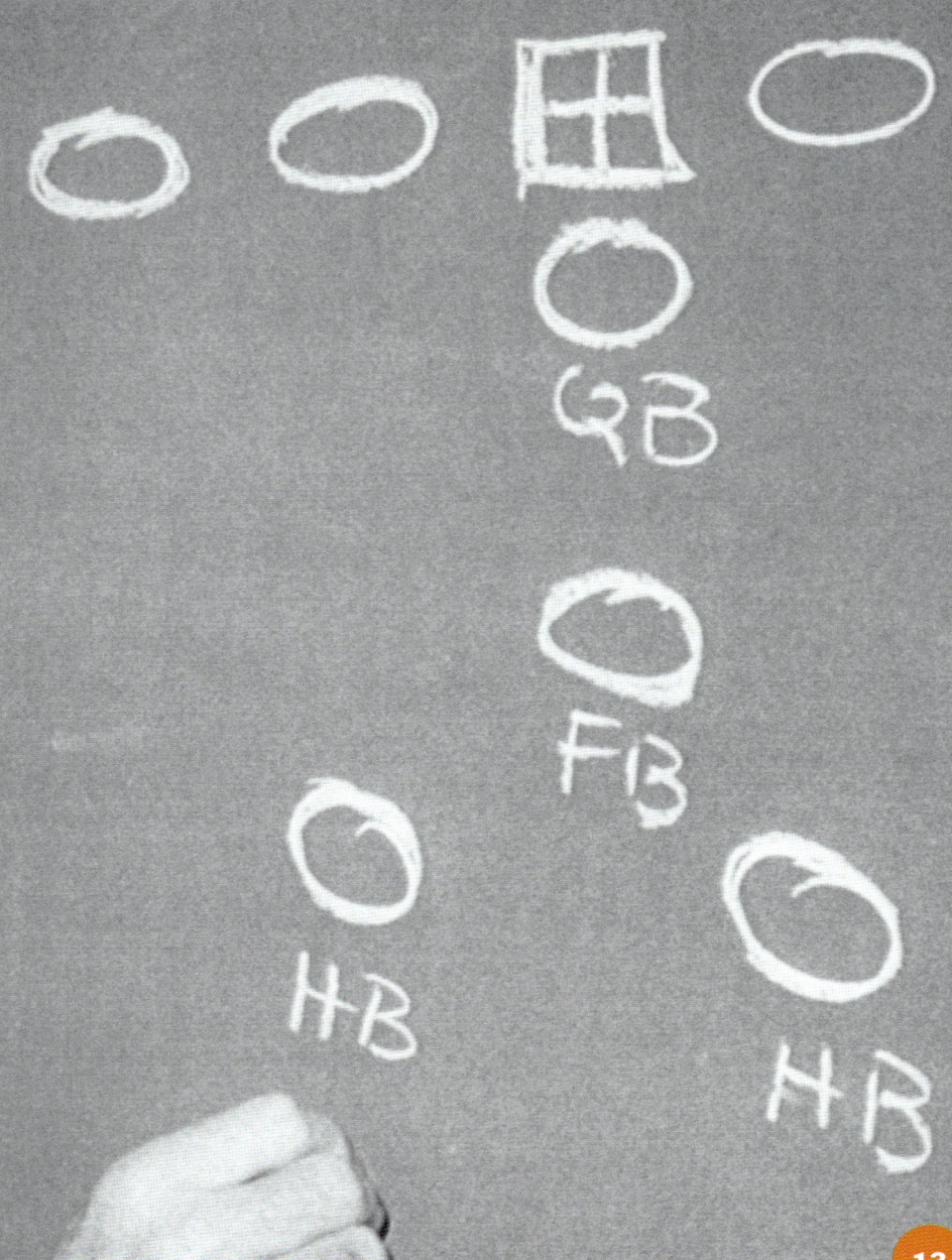

QB

FB

HB   HB

Texas running back Jim Bertelsen scores the winning touchdown in a 1969 game against Arkansas.

In 1963, the Longhorns dominated. They finished the year 11–0. That secured the team's first national title.

In 1969, Texas and Arkansas met as the country's top two teams. Arkansas went up 14–0. Then Texas rallied to win 15–14. Soon after, the Longhorns won their second national title. The following year, they won their third.

Defensive back Jerry Gray was one of the best Longhorns of the 1980s.

Royal stepped down after the 1976 season. Texas still had plenty of talent. The Longhorns went 11–1 in 1977. Their only loss came in the Cotton Bowl. Texas remained a top program through the 1980s. And in the 1990s, the Longhorns became known for their explosive offenses.

THIRD STRING

In a 1977 game, Texas lost its first two quarterbacks against Oklahoma. Third-stringer Randy McEachern was ready. He led the Longhorns to a 13–6 win. McEachern kept the starting job after that.

PLAYER SPOTLIGHT

EARL CAMPBELL

Earl Campbell was big and fast. That was a dangerous combination for a running back. Defenders seemed to bounce off him. Campbell starred for the Longhorns in 1974 and 1975. Injuries limited him the next year. But he was dominant as a senior.

Campbell rushed for 1,744 yards in 1977. He also scored 19 touchdowns. His play helped Texas go 11–1. Campbell became Texas's first Heisman Trophy winner. That award is given to college football's best player.

> **EARL CAMPBELL RAN FOR 4,443 YARDS IN HIS FOUR YEARS WITH THE LONGHORNS.**

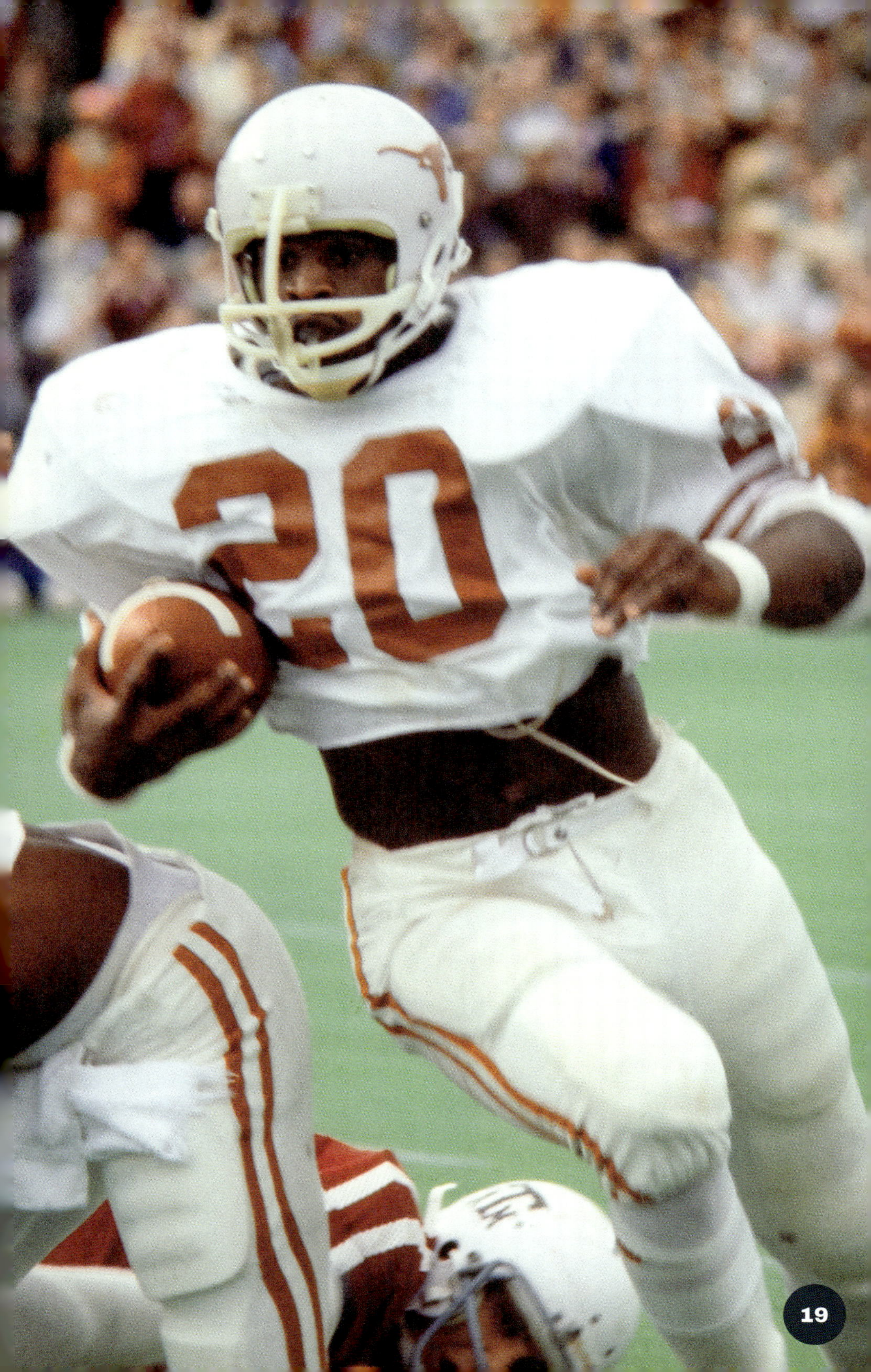

CHAPTER 3

LEGENDS

In 1939, Texas trailed Arkansas by six points late in the game. Running back Jack Crain scored on a 67-yard touchdown catch. Then he kicked the winning extra point. Crain went on to become Texas's first two-time All-American.

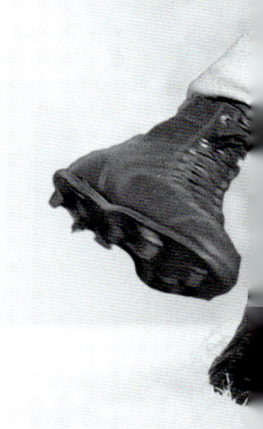

Jack Crain was the first Texas player to run for more than 1,000 yards in his career.

Bobby Layne starred as Texas's quarterback from 1944 to 1947. He earned all-conference honors all four years. Layne also won a lot of big games. The biggest was the Cotton Bowl in the 1946 season. Texas scored six touchdowns. Layne threw for two. He ran for three. He also caught one. Texas thumped Missouri 40–27.

TWO-WAY STAR

Lineman Bud McFadin played offense and defense for Texas. He left the school as an all-time great. McFadin earned All-America honors in 1949 and 1950.

Bobby Layne also served as a punter for the Longhorns.

Scott Appleton was a tackling machine. The defensive lineman played a big role in Texas's 1963 national title. Tommy Nobis shined that year, too. And he was only getting started. Nobis was a good linebacker. But he was also named the nation's best offensive lineman in 1965.

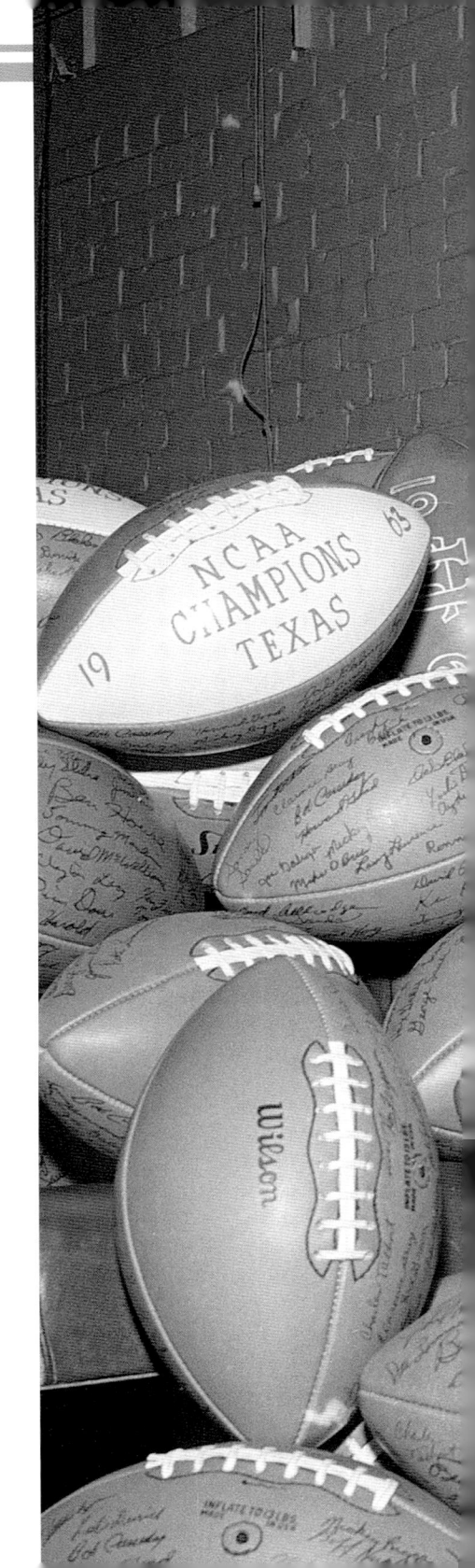

Scott Appleton takes some time off from tackling to sign footballs.

Roosevelt Leaks (46) ran for more than 1,400 yards in 1973.

For many years, Texas did not allow Black players. That began to change in the late 1960s. Running back Roosevelt Leaks was one of the team's first Black stars. In 1973, he became the Longhorns' first Black All-American.

Brad Shearer and Steve McMichael were powerful defensive linemen. They piled up tackles in the 1970s.

SHUTDOWN DB

Jerry Gray led Texas's defense in the early 1980s. The defensive back was known for his ferocity. He could shut down even the most skilled opponents.

PLAYER SPOTLIGHT

RICKY WILLIAMS

In the 1970s, Earl Campbell set a high standard for Texas running backs. In the 1990s, Ricky Williams raised it even higher. Williams started strong in 1995 and 1996. Then he exploded in his final two seasons.

Williams was both powerful and fast. He could bulldoze through defenses. He led the nation in rushing yards and touchdowns in 1997. He did it again in 1998. Williams ended his career with 21 college records. He also won the 1998 Heisman Trophy.

> **IN HIS FOUR YEARS WITH TEXAS, RICKY WILLIAMS SCORED 75 TOUCHDOWNS.**

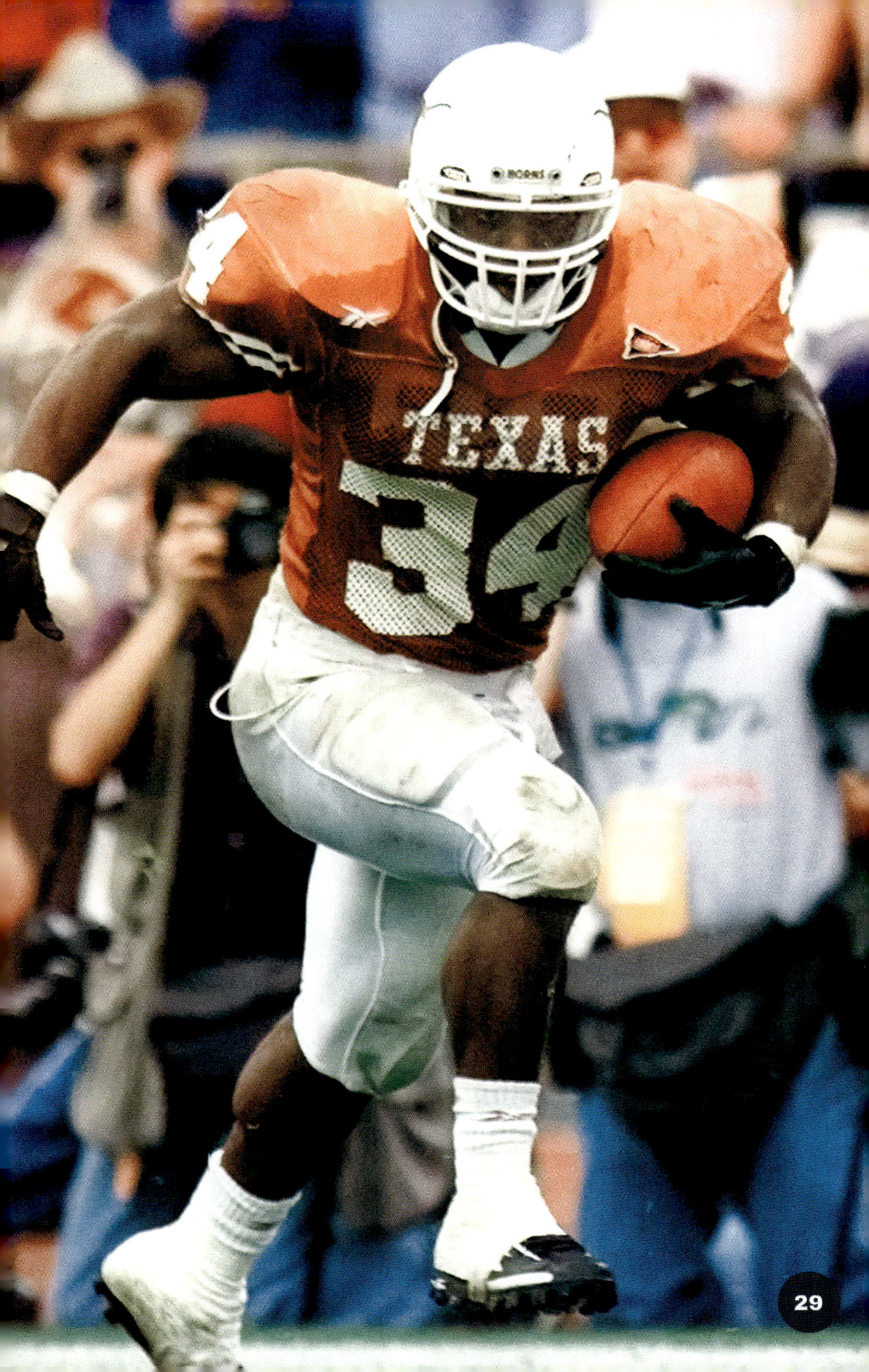
TEXAS
34

CHAPTER 4
RECENT HISTORY

The Longhorns had a tough year in 1997. Mack Brown got them back on track. He took over as coach in 1998. His 2004 team reached the Rose Bowl. A thrilling win over Michigan proved that Texas was a top team once again.

Longhorns kicker Dusty Mangum (14) nails a field goal as time expires, lifting Texas to a 38–37 win over Michigan in the Rose Bowl.

In the 2005 season, the Longhorns went undefeated. They faced USC in the national title game. It became an instant classic. USC was the defending champion. But Texas showed no fear. The teams traded scores all game long. USC led 38–33 in the final minute. But with 19 seconds to go, Texas quarterback Vince Young ran for a touchdown. The Longhorns were national champions!

> **Vince Young scores the winning touchdown to give the Longhorns their fourth national title.**

Texas quarterback Colt McCoy looks for a receiver during a 2008 game against Oklahoma.

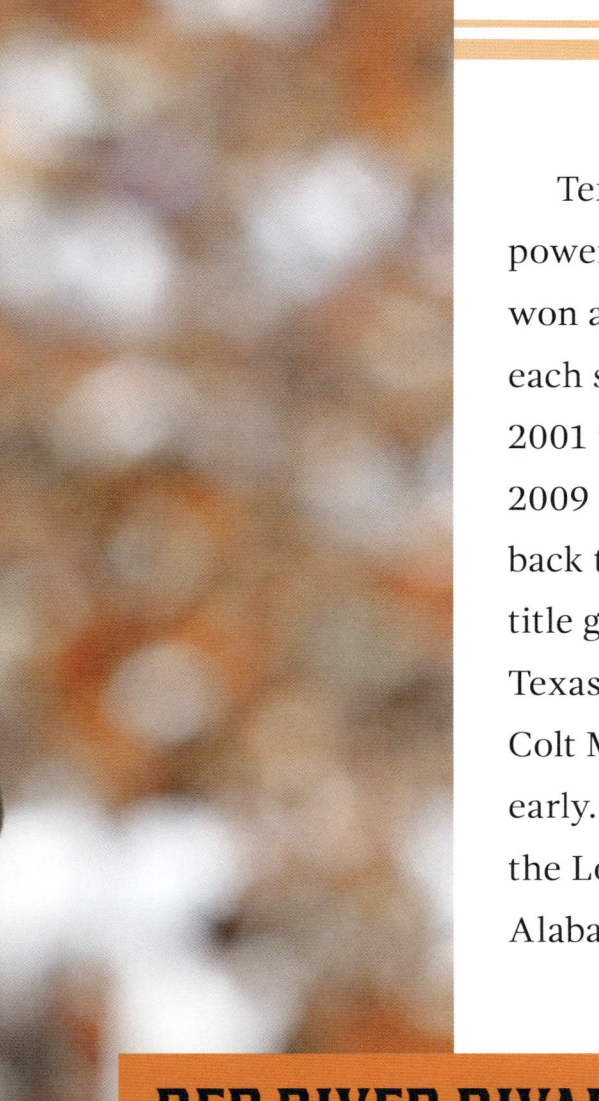

Texas remained a power. The Longhorns won at least 10 games each season from 2001 to 2009. The 2009 team made it back to the national title game. However, Texas quarterback Colt McCoy got hurt early. Without him, the Longhorns fell to Alabama 37–21.

RED RIVER RIVALRY

The Red River separates Texas and Oklahoma. So, when those two teams play, it's known as the Red River Rivalry. The 2008 game turned into a shootout. Top-ranked Oklahoma led by 11 points. But Colt McCoy led a comeback. No. 5 Texas pulled off a 45–35 win.

Running back Jaydon Blue carries the ball during a 2024 win over Kentucky.

Mack Brown left after the 2013 season. The team cycled through coaches. Finally, in 2023, the Longhorns took a big step. A win at third-ranked Alabama showed Texas could contend again. The Longhorns reached the playoff that season. And in 2024, they reached the playoff again. The future looked bright in Texas.

GOING BOWLING

In the 2024 season, the playoff expanded to 12 teams. So, some teams played in two bowl games that season. Texas was one of them. The Longhorns beat Arizona State 39–31 in the Peach Bowl. The next week, they fell to Ohio State 28–14 in the Cotton Bowl.

CHAPTER 5

MODERN STARS

The Longhorns were loaded with talent in the early 2000s. Roy Williams set several team receiving records. Cedric Benson was named the nation's top running back in 2004. That same year, linebacker Derrick Johnson took home top defensive player honors.

Roy Williams piled up 3,866 receiving yards from 2000 to 2003.

In 2005, a new group took Texas to the next level. Dual-threat quarterback Vince Young led the way. He was the Heisman Trophy runner-up. Safety Michael Huff II dominated on defense. He helped make a key stop in the national title game.

TOP DEFENDER

Freshman Brian Orakpo was a backup on Texas's 2005 team. The powerful defensive end blossomed after that. In 2008, he was named the nation's top defensive player.

Michael Huff II blocks a punt during a 2003 game against Kansas State.

Jordan Shipley hauls in a touchdown catch during a 2008 game against Florida Atlantic.

42

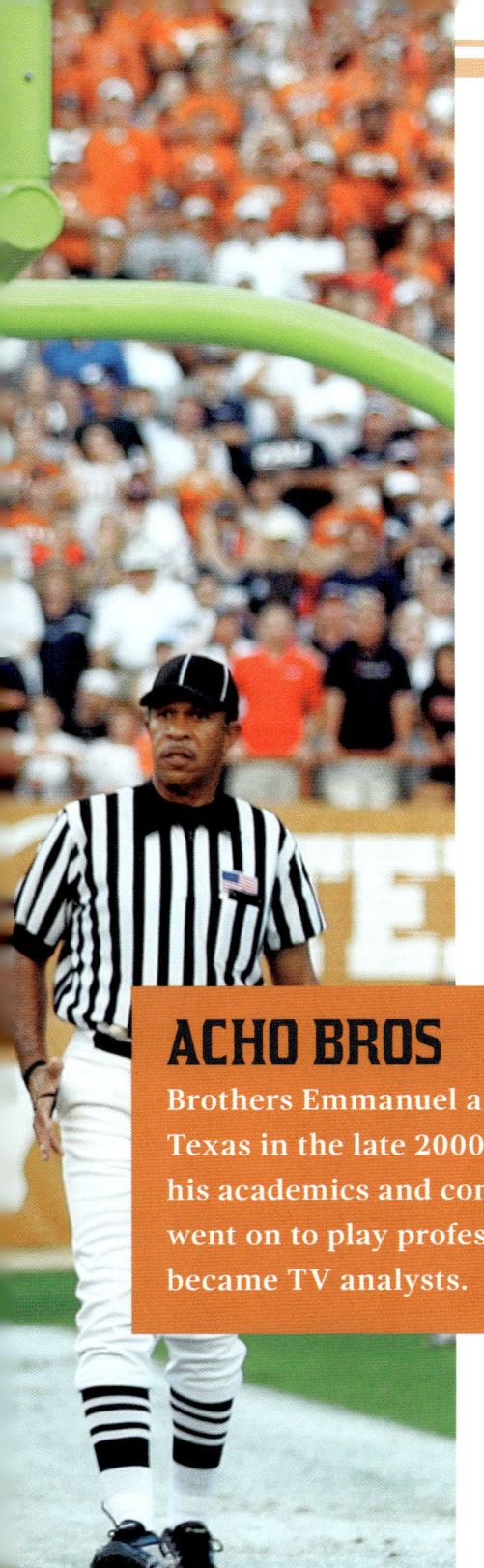

Colt McCoy and Jordan Shipley were a powerful combination. The quarterback-receiver duo always seemed to connect. They helped Texas reach the national title game. Both set records for their position.

ACHO BROS

Brothers Emmanuel and Sam Acho starred at Texas in the late 2000s. Sam was honored for his academics and community service. Both went on to play professionally. They later became TV analysts.

In three seasons, Quinn Ewers threw 68 touchdown passes.

Texas kept producing star players. D'Onta Foreman was named the nation's top running back in 2016. Bijan Robinson earned the same honor in 2022. Quinn Ewers emerged as one of the nation's best quarterbacks in 2023. In 2024, he shared duties with Arch Manning.

STOPPING THE RUN

Running against the Longhorns was difficult in 2023. So was scoring. Defensive tackle T'Vondre Sweat was a big reason why. He was named the nation's top defensive lineman.

PLAYER SPOTLIGHT

VINCE YOUNG

Nothing terrified defenders like Vince Young with the football. The quarterback stood 6-foot-5 (196 cm). He weighed 233 pounds (106 kg). Young could sling passes all over the field. He could also take off running.

Young's 2005 season was his best. He passed for more than 3,000 yards. He also ran for more than 1,000. That had never been done before. Young delivered another amazing performance in the national title game. He ran for 200 yards and three touchdowns. He led Texas to a thrilling 41–38 victory.

VINCE YOUNG TOPPED 6,000 PASSING YARDS IN HIS THREE YEARS AT TEXAS.

47

CHAPTER 6

TEAM TRIVIA

In 1900, the University of Texas took a poll. It asked students to pick the school's colors. Voters picked orange and white. However, the shade of orange changed over the years. In 1967, Texas settled on burnt orange. The school is now famous for using that color.

Texas home games feature a sea of burnt orange.

Smokey the Cannon is fired every time the Longhorns score.

50

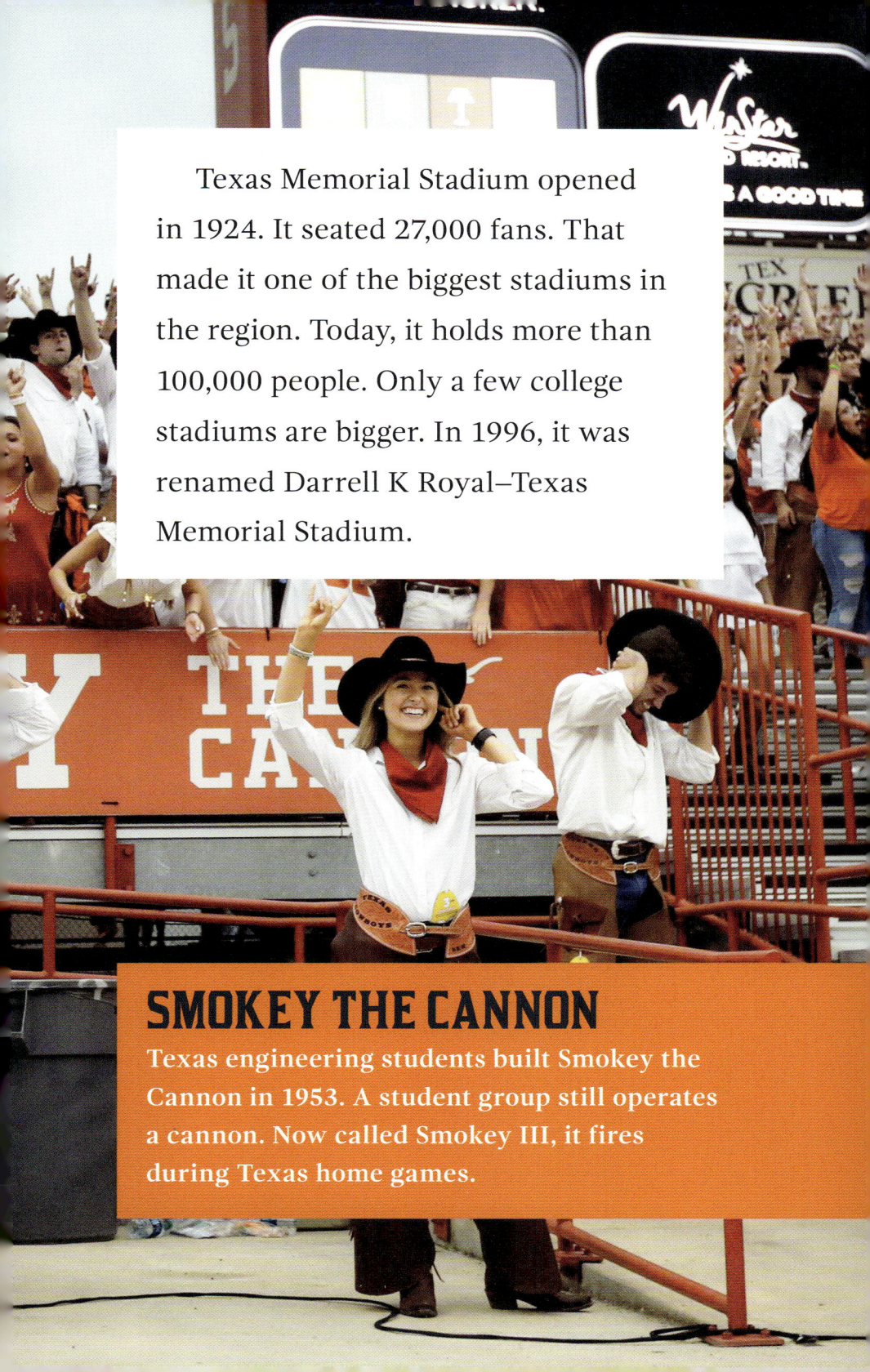

Texas Memorial Stadium opened in 1924. It seated 27,000 fans. That made it one of the biggest stadiums in the region. Today, it holds more than 100,000 people. Only a few college stadiums are bigger. In 1996, it was renamed Darrell K Royal–Texas Memorial Stadium.

SMOKEY THE CANNON
Texas engineering students built Smokey the Cannon in 1953. A student group still operates a cannon. Now called Smokey III, it fires during Texas home games.

Texas fans were in for a surprise in 1916. The Longhorns were playing Texas A&M. At halftime, an alum brought a live longhorn steer onto the field. The animal was nicknamed Bevo. Other longhorns have taken over as Bevo over the years. The mascot remains a beloved part of Texas home games.

BIG BERTHA

Five members of the Longhorn Band have a special job at Texas games. They manage Big Bertha. At 500 pounds (227 kg), it is the world's largest bass drum.

Bevo enters the stadium before a 2019 game against Oklahoma State.

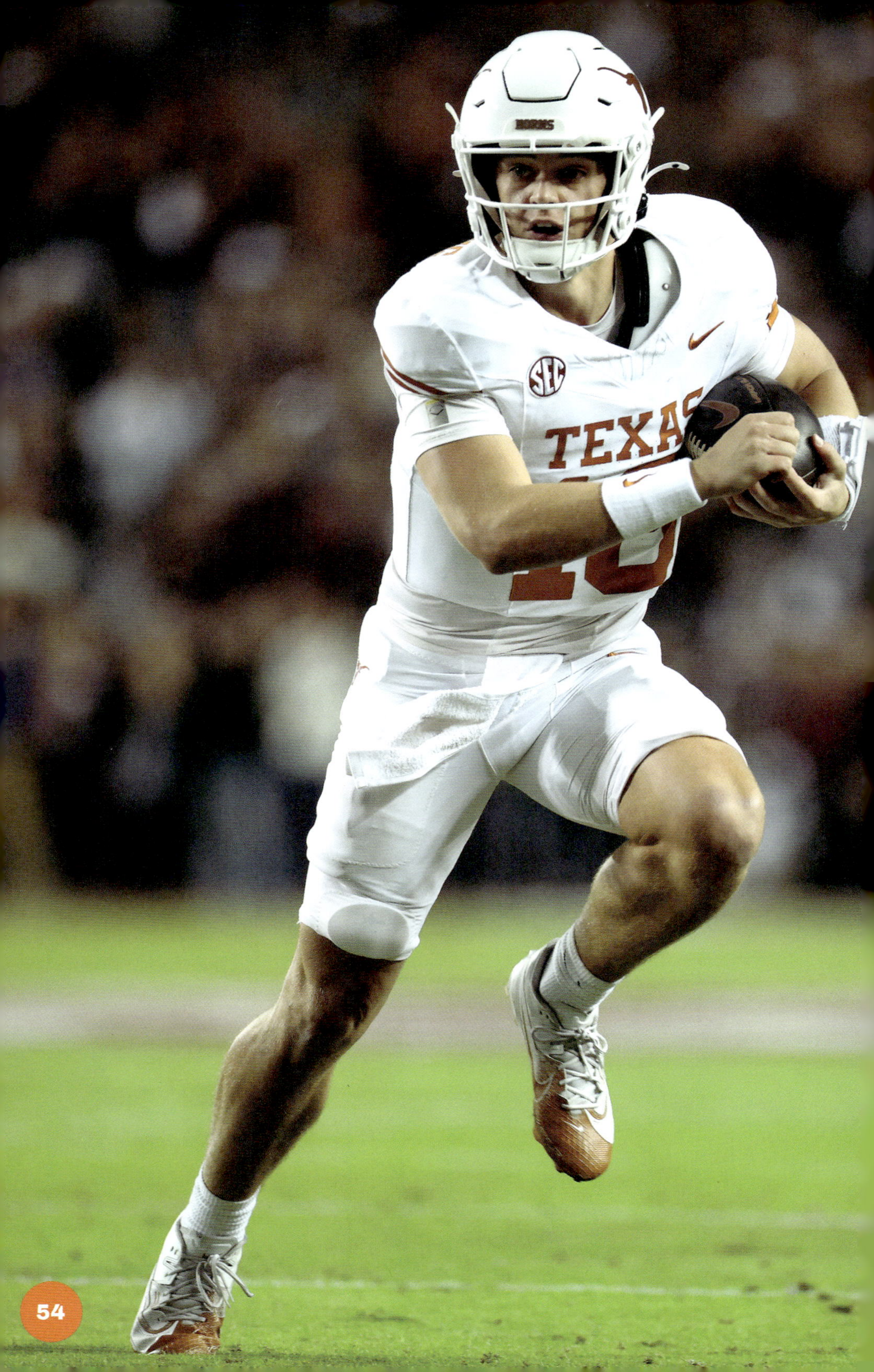
SEC
TEXAS

Texas and Texas A&M battle for bragging rights in the Lone Star Showdown. The teams met 118 times between 1894 and 2011. After that, they played in different conferences for several years. But the rivalry resumed in 2024. Texas won 17–7.

The Red River Rivalry began in 1900. Since 1929, Texas and Oklahoma have played each other every year. It's often one of the biggest games of the season.

Quarterback Arch Manning scores a touchdown during a 2024 win over Texas A&M.

TEAM RECORDS

All-Time Passing Yards: 13,253
Colt McCoy (2006–09)

All-Time Rushing Yards: 6,279
Ricky Williams (1995–98)

All-Time Receiving Yards: 3,866
Roy Williams (2000–03)

All-Time Touchdowns: 75
Ricky Williams (1995–98)

All-Time Scoring: 452
Ricky Williams (1995–98)

All-Time Interceptions: 17
Nathan Vasher (2000–03), Noble Doss (1939–41)

All-Time Sacks: 40.5
Kiki DeAyala (1979–82)

All-Time Coaching Wins: 167
Darrell K Royal (1957–76)

Heisman Trophy Winners: 2
Earl Campbell (1977), Ricky Williams (1998)

National Championships: 4
1963, 1969, 1970†, 2005

† Season in which more than one school claims the national title.

All statistics are accurate through 2024.

57

TIMELINE

1893 — On November 30, Texas plays its first-ever football game and beats Dallas University 18–16.

1924 — On November 8, the first game is held at what is now Darrell K Royal–Texas Memorial Stadium.

1943 — On January 1, Texas wins its first bowl game by beating Georgia Tech 14–7 in the Cotton Bowl.

1955 — Cheerleader Harley Clark invents the "Hook 'em Horns" hand symbol.

1963 — No. 2 Texas beats No. 1 Oklahoma on the way to the Longhorns' first national championship.

1969 · 1971 · 1977 · 1998 · 2006

1971: On January 1, Texas falls to Notre Dame in the Cotton Bowl but is still named national champion after going 10–0 during the regular season.

1998: Running back Ricky Williams is named Texas's second Heisman Trophy winner.

1969: No. 1 Texas comes back from down 14–0 to beat No. 2 Arkansas 15–14. The Longhorns go on to win another national title.

1977: Running back Earl Campbell becomes the first Texas player to win the Heisman Trophy.

2006: On January 4, quarterback Vince Young leads Texas past USC at the Rose Bowl to claim the Longhorns' fourth national title.

59

COMPREHENSION QUESTIONS

Write your answers on a separate piece of paper.

1. Write a paragraph that explains the main ideas of Chapter 2.

2. Who do you think was the greatest player in Texas Longhorns history? Why?

3. Which coach led Texas to its first bowl game?
    - A. Dana X. Bible
    - B. Darrell K Royal
    - C. Mack Brown

4. What hurt Texas's chances of winning the national title in the 2009 season?
    - A. The game was played at Alabama's home stadium.
    - B. The team didn't have its starting quarterback for most of the game.
    - C. Texas coach Mack Brown was sick and had to miss the game.

5. What does **rallied** mean in this book?

   *Arkansas went up 14–0. Then Texas **rallied** to win 15–14.*

       A. came from behind
       B. lost by a wide margin
       C. replaced all its players

6. What does **resumed** mean in this book?

   *The teams met 118 times between 1894 and 2011. After that, they played in different conferences for several years. But the rivalry **resumed** in 2024. Texas won 17–7.*

       A. ended forever
       B. lost a game
       C. started again

Answer key on page 64.

GLOSSARY

All-American
A player named as one of the best in the country in his or her sport.

alum
A person who graduated from a certain school.

bowl game
A postseason college football game that successful teams are invited to take part in.

conference
A group of teams that make up part of a sports league.

dual-threat
Able to throw and run as a quarterback.

expanded
Became larger.

mascot
A figure that is the symbol of a sports team.

rivalry
An ongoing competition that brings out strong emotion from fans and players.

snap
The start of each play, when the center passes the ball back to the quarterback.

tradition
A way of doing something that is passed down over many years.

TO LEARN MORE

BOOKS

Kelley, K. C. *Texas Longhorns*. The Child's World, 2022.

Meier, William. *Texas Longhorns*. Abdo Publishing, 2021.

Temple, Ramey. *Texas Longhorns*. AV2 by Weigl, 2020.

ONLINE RESOURCES

Visit **www.apexeditions.com** to find links and resources related to this title.

ABOUT THE AUTHOR

Derek Moon is an author and avid Stratego player who lives in Watertown, Massachusetts, with his wife and daughter.

INDEX

Appleton, Scott, 24

Benson, Cedric, 38
Bible, Dana X., 11
Brown, Mack, 31, 37

Campbell, Earl, 18, 28
Cotton Bowl, 17, 22, 37
Crain, Jack, 20

Darrell K Royal–Texas
   Memorial Stadium, 51

Ewers, Quinn, 45

Foreman, D'Onta, 45

Heisman Trophy, 18, 28, 40, 46,
Huff, Michael II, 40

Johnson, Derrick, 38

Layne, Bobby, 22
Leaks, Roosevelt, 27
Longhorn Band, 5, 52

Manning, Arch, 45
McCoy, Colt, 35, 43
McMichael, Steve, 27

Nobis, Tommy, 24

Red River Rivalry, 35, 55
Robinson, Bijan, 45
Rose Bowl, 31
Royal, Darell K, 12, 17

Shearer, Brad, 27
Shipley, Jordan, 43
Smokey the Cannon, 51

Williams, Ricky, 28
Williams, Roy, 38

Young, Vince, 32, 40, 46

ANSWER KEY:
1. Answers will vary; 2. Answers will vary; 3. A; 4. B; 5. A; 6. C